# Life Lessons from the Chocolate Factory

## 10 Rich, Satisfying Nuggets To Nibble On

Christopher Holl

A.J. Neal Publishing

# Life Lessons from the Chocolate Factory
## 10 Rich, Satisfying Nuggets to Nibble On

## Christopher Holl

Published by A.J. Neal Publishing
Post Office Box 1469
Jackson, NJ 08527

Copyediting and Interior Layout: Lynette M. Smith
Cover Design: Jenni Wheeler

Print edition ISBN: 9780985144234
Electronic edition ISBN: 9780985144203
First Printing 2012
Library of Congress Control Number: 2012934928

Selected passages were quoted from the movie *Willy Wonka & the Chocolate Factory* (1971). The author of *Life Lessons from the Chocolate Factory* has no affiliation with or connection to the producers or owners of the motion picture.

To my wife Gina, and to my children Carmella, Christina, Teresa and Christopher.

# Contents

# Introduction

"Willy Wonka is on, Willy Wonka is on!" I yelled while darting down the stairs of our shingled New Jersey bi-level home, scrambling to the TV room, hoping to secure a prized couch end before one of my four siblings did. Growing up in the 1970s, this was the one day of the year when my favorite movie, *Willy Wonka & the Chocolate Factory,* was on TV. This was a big event! Back then, things like Netflix, YouTube, Hulu and the Internet didn't exist. Television had only seven channels and a station did not feature a movie for an entire week as is sometimes done today. You had to know the time and channel when your favorite movie was on or you wouldn't see it again for another year!

Released in 1971, this family musical is based on the Roald Dahl book, *Charlie and the Chocolate Factory.* Who can forget the mysterious, reclusive and eccentric chocolate maker, Willy Wonka, brilliantly played by Gene Wilder? And what children watching the movie didn't suspend reality and dream of winning the lifetime supply of Wonka chocolate by drawing one of the five golden tickets themselves! We learn that Wonka's real motivation is to find a trusted heir to his magnificent empire and ensure that his scary, scar-faced arch enemy, Slugworth, does not steal his secrets, especially the everlasting gobstopper. The event becomes a worldwide phenomenon, and a comical hysteria encompasses the globe as everyone searches for an elusive golden ticket.

The children who discovered the tickets made quite an impression on me. With the exception of Charlie, who is considerate and well mannered, they are all spoiled, self-indulgent, insufferable brats. Augustus Gloop is a gluttonous serial eater whose equally ravenous father devours the microphone of a reporter during an interview! Violet Beauregarde is destined to grow up and be that loud, bossy, gum-chomping neighbor or coworker nobody can stand. Veruka Salt is a wealthy, catered-to peanut heiress and reminder of the cousin you dreaded visiting as a kid because you couldn't touch any of her toys. And let's not forget about Mike Teavee, the obnoxious TV addict who lives in a fantasy world and has no time for the real people in his life, who want to be part of it, like his family.

With their parents and grandparent in tow, they set off on the first Saturday in October to Wonka's factory to claim the coveted prize. As the tour gets underway, four of the children, consumed by their own immediate desires and excessive attachment to the wrong things, choose to violate Wonka's rules of conduct and are ejected from the factory. Augustus falls into the chocolate river while trying to drink it, Violet blows up into a blueberry for chewing the three course dinner gum, Veruka registers as a bad egg on the "eggdicator" and is dropped into the trash and Mike shrinks himself to the size of an index finger with the Wonkavision machine. Even Charlie shows some uncharacteristic lack of control and helps himself to fizzy lifting drink. With each child's shameful exit, the Oompa Loompas, little people with orange skin and bushy white eyebrows who work at the factory, sing a song of cautionary advice to those remaining.

# Why I Wrote This Book

I rediscovered *Willy Wonka & the Chocolate Factory* years later as a father, when I purchased the 25-year anniversary edition (on VHS!) and watched it with my daughters. I was struck by the moral decision Charlie later makes in the film as more than just a dramatic moment. As kids will do with a movie, we watched it over and over again and I saw that other "life lessons" dotted the movie's landscape. I began to point them out to my girls, sometimes putting the movie on pause to make a point (not always welcomed). Thus, *Life Lessons from the Chocolate Factory* unwraps enduring nuggets of non-caloric wisdom, as relevant today as in the past.

You can argue that "there's nothing new under the sun" when it comes to the great principles of how we should live our lives. It was the ancient Greek philosopher Socrates who said, "It is not living that matters, but living rightly." Hard not to agree with, yet we all struggle with the living rightly part. But we journey on, thankfully choosing right more often than not, but still stumbling along the way. For those moments, I hope what's in these pages can act as a source of inspiration and some wind at your back to help get you to a place you want to be.

Although this book draws lessons from the movie, the narrative is not restricted to just the film. Sprinkled throughout are supporting perspectives discerned from observations of our culture, other movies, television, psychology and a few personal vignettes. For those in your 30s, 40s and older, it may sometimes act as a serendipitous walk down Memory Lane. If you're younger, what's lost in nostalgia will hopefully be found in an insight from the example itself. Collectively, I hope it all works to inspire you to find, or rediscover, a few life-living and life-giving nuggets—ones as satisfying as your favorite piece of chocolate, but with a peace-of-mind benefit that lasts long after the first bite!

# Lesson One

## Moments of Decision

*Some choices we live not only once but a thousand times
over, remembering them for the rest of our lives.*
—Richard Bach

Moment of decision. In an instant, a conscious choice
is made, a deliberate path taken. What we decide to do
in this frozen moment in time could very well impact
the rest of our lives, and the lives of those around us—
for better, or for worse. Forever. And it can all happen
in the blink of an eye.

One of the last scenes in the movie illustrates this.
The tour is over and only Charlie and Grandpa Joe
remain, the other children having all been eliminated
because of their rude and selfish ways. Grandpa Joe
asks Wonka what's next.

Wonka brushes them off quickly, bemoaning how
the whole day has been wasted as he retreats to his

office. Perplexed, they follow him into the bizarre "half" office, furnished with fixtures and furniture items that have been cut in half. The decor serves to reinforce Wonka's eccentricity. Hunched over his half desk, the room is silent, save for the loud ticking of the half wall clock. When Grandpa Joe asks about the lifetime supply of chocolate, Wonka immediately shuts him down and reveals he knows they broke the rules when they stole fizzy lifting drink (a beverage that lifts you into the air).

Wonka then launches into his "you get nothing" tirade, screaming at them both, his straggly, unkempt hair bouncing up and down with each declaration.

> Wrong, Sir, wrong! Under Section 37 B of the contract signed by him, it states quite clearly that all offers shall become null and void if, and you can read it for yourself in this photostatic copy, "I, the undersigned, shall forfeit all rights, privileges, and licenses herein and herein contained, et cetera, et cetera... fax mentis incendium gloria culpum, et cetera, et cetera... memo bis punitor delicatum!" It's all there, black and white, clear as crystal! You stole fizzy lifting drinks. You bumped into the ceiling which now has to be washed and sterilized, so you get nothing! You lose! Good day, Sir!

Stunned, Grandpa Joe yells back and accuses him of being a crook and a cheat.

Charlie stands there, his mouth agape, sullen, dejected, his dream shattered in a thousand and one pieces. You would think the grandfather would be the mature one, comforting the boy and reassuring him that everything would be all right. That doesn't happen, though. In fact, quite the opposite. He takes Charlie by the arm and ushers him out the door. "Come on, Charlie, let's get out of here. I'll get even with him if it's the last thing I ever do. If Slugworth wants a gobstopper, he'll get one."

Slugworth is Wonka's competitor and archenemy. During the tour, Wonka made the children promise when he gave them his most secret and prized creation—the everlasting gobstopper—that they would never let Slugworth get hold of it. Charlie knew how much Slugworth wanted it, too. Because upon finding the last golden ticket, he made Charlie a generous offer to give him the prized confection in exchange for enough money to take care of Charlie and his family for the rest of their lives. Pretty tempting offer, especially when one is desperately poor like Charlie.

What a position Charlie finds himself in at that moment. Clenching the everlasting gobstopper in his hand, he has the means to "get even" and bring down Wonka and his empire. What power, and it all rests with him! And why shouldn't he, for the way he was just treated? It's true that he and Grandpa lingered behind during the tour and, when no one was around, drank the fizzy lifting drink, but that shouldn't disqualify him. He wasn't nearly as bad as the other selfish, nasty children. Hey, he had worked hard for his golden ticket, expected more, wanted more. He thought he was entitled—and this wasn't fair. Not fair at all.

Thus, the time has come—it's a moment of decision for Charlie. Little does he know the course of events this decisive moment will set off. (Who ever knows?) Stopping briefly as Grandpa Joe ushers him out the door, he looks at Wonka, pauses and then walks back to him. "Mr. Wonka," he says, and quietly places the everlasting gobstopper on his desk, then turns and walks away. He could have walked out the door with his grandfather and an attitude and desire bent on revenge. But he chose not to. Not only that, but Charlie backs up his decision with an action to guarantee it is carried out—he gives back the gobstopper that Slugworth would use to ruin Wonka. He says no to the temptation to be his worst self, however satisfying and "delicious" it might be in the moment. And what was the result?

Wonka places his hand over the gobstopper. "So shines a good deed in a weary world. Charlie... my boy... you won! You did it! You did it! I knew you would, I just knew you would."

Not only did Charlie win the lifetime supply of chocolate, but because his "moment of decision" was rooted in doing the right thing, despite the hurt and rejection he felt, Wonka decides to give him the entire chocolate factory itself!

All too often, we hear stories of politicians, celebrities and athletes "messing up" in the public square. Tweeting this inappropriate picture or texting that depraved stream of consciousness. Saying yes to things they know should be no. Making choices that compromise their integrity and put them in the middle of a self-created scandal. In short, bad decisions, made in a second of time. The only difference between us and those in the public spotlight is that our bad decisions are not splashed across the cover of *People* magazine or featured on gossip TV (thankfully).

But wise decisions can be made in the same moment too. Like Charlie's. Wise decisions, even difficult ones, don't weigh us down long term. Wise decision making considers where a decision places us in the moment and potentially in the future. It's like a skilled pool player who, when making a shot, is concerned with not only pocketing the ball, but where the cue ball will be positioned for the next try. Or the chess player who is thinking two or three moves ahead with each turn.

## Can the Flap of a Butterfly's Wings in Brazil Set off a Tornado in Texas?

How in the world does this tie in with lessons from the movie? Something always happens on the other side of a decision, like we saw with Charlie's. This story underscores how something, even a minor event, can significantly impact the course of other events that follow it.

Working as a professor in MIT's department of meteorology in the 1960s, Edward Lorenz accidently discovered that slight alterations in the initial conditions of weather patterns could, over time, produce completely different weather scenarios. This discovery came about when he reran a simple weather simulation and left the last few digits off one of the variables. As the story goes, Lorenz went to get a cup of coffee and upon his return found that the repeated, slightly altered experiment had generated a vastly different weather pattern. This eventually became known as the "butterfly effect," a popular way of describing unpredictability and illustrating how small events can result in large, widespread consequences.

Hence, the flapping of a butterfly's fragile wings in the early stages of a weather system can create a tiny change in the atmosphere, setting off a chain reaction that causes a major event far away, like a tornado.

*Can create.* Had the spoiled children not behaved so terribly or Charlie not so nobly, the movie might have had a completely different outcome. We never know exactly how our choices create variables in our "life system" but, like Lorenz's butterfly wings, they do change things. Maybe big, maybe small, maybe not even noticeable. But unlike Lorenz, we don't have the benefit of predictive computer modeling to know how our decisions will shape the future. They could result in the equivalent of a tornado in our lives, in a beautiful, long-range forecast or maybe the keys to a chocolate factory! If there's going to be a butterfly effect in your life, and there will, endeavor to make it work for you.

## The Domino Effect

As a kid, I didn't know about Lorenz's research, but did know about dominos. My siblings and I loved to line up dozens of domino pieces in an intricate design, tip one over to begin the fall and watch with amusement until none were left standing. As an adult, I know that decisions follow a similar pattern. One decision, made in a moment's time, like the tipping of a single domino, can leave marks far beyond the initial fall. Either good, or not so good. One or the other— there are no neutral decisions. There is always impact.

I suspect Charlie did not consciously think about the domino effect or the flapping of a butterfly's wings when he returned the gobstopper. But he had a conscience and sense of right and wrong. And probably a sense of his own weakness. He made, as Stephen Covey describes it, a principle-based decision. Such moments of decision may not always result in winning the equivalent of a chocolate factory but could prevent a meltdown somewhere along the way!

## Houdini Could Not Escape Consequences

Here's another way of thinking about the impact of decisions. When a stone is dropped into a lake, ripples are a predictable outcome. The ripple effect of decisions are consequences. Familiar with Harry Houdini? He was the famed magician of the early 20th century, an expert in escaping from virtually any situation. He awed crowds around the world by escaping from handcuffs, leg irons, straightjackets, packing crates and prisons. Simply put, he could escape from anything. I would wager, however, that if Mr. Houdini was bound or shackled by consequences, it would be one feat he could not emerge victorious from!

Whether we believe in consequences or not, whether we give them much thought at all, doesn't matter. Consequences happen. The key is to think about the domino effect—and to make sure that the cascade effect of our decisions will, like strategically placed dominos, fall in place the way we would like them to.

## Toss the Temptation

Not only did Charlie choose to do the right thing by not helping Slugworth and bringing Wonka down, but he backed it up with an action that would guarantee his decision would be carried out—he got rid of the temptation, his ticket to "getting even" with someone who just hurt him—by giving back the everlasting gobstopper. He walked away—completely—from any chance of going back on his decision. And because of that decision, made in a moment of time, based on principle and backed up with action, his life was about to change, for the good, forever.

## morsels to munch on

◈ Base decisions on principles, not circumstances. Principles don't change.

◈ Beware of the "butterfly effect" that comes with every decision.

◈ You can run, and you can hide—but not from consequences.

## Lesson Two

## All I Have to Do Is Dream—Not!

*If you have built castles in the air, your work need not be lost; that is where they should be. Now put the foundations under them.*

—Carl Jung

Charlie dreams about winning a golden ticket more than anything else. He thinks and talks about finding the rare ticket all day and again in the evening as he goes to bed and drifts off to sleep. He seems to think that if he only dreams about it hard enough, it will happen.

His fantasy is encouraged by Grandpa Joe, who, when Charlie opens a Wonka Bar and asks if he has a chance, responds, "You've got more, Charlie, because you want it more."

But beyond purchasing a few Wonka Bars, Charlie sits idle, allowing his dream to become subject to the whims of fate, versus having faith in himself to do something about it.

## I Can Make You Mine Anytime, Night or Day

Recorded by The Everly Brothers in 1958 and considered among the greatest songs of all time, "All I Have to Do Is Dream" plays to the heartstrings of a young man, resigned that he can only dream about being with the woman he loves. Despite his resignation, he finds some comfort in the fantasy that he can have her in his arms, with all her charms, because all he has to do is "dream, dream, dream."

A pretty disappointing approach to life, though, isn't it? The young man in the song makes no attempt to pursue his dream girl, to approach her, talk to her, make a connection or start a friendship. No, he is on the sidelines, at a safe distance, hoping that "fate" will somehow strike in a good way. For a brief moment, though, he realizes the futility of his actions:

"I can make you mine, taste your lips of wine, anytime night or day. Only trouble is, gee whiz, I'm dreamin' my life away."

Unfortunately, although he realizes he is dreaming his life away, he goes right back to it, and that is how the song concludes. And let's face it—too often we go back to the dreaming and meaning-to-do-something cycle—dreaming and meaning, dreaming and meaning, dreaming and meaning.

Wonka is a dreamer too. But he turns his dreams into realities, and says as much as he leads the group into the chocolate room of the factory. "Inside this room, all of my dreams become realities. And some of my realities become dreams." I can imagine the late Steve Jobs, one of the great visionaries and inventors of our time, saying something similar (and believing it). When a dream wakes you up, it's time to get out of bed and get working on it.

## I'll Sleep on It

More than an expression, "I'll sleep on it" can provide a temporary excuse to hover in the dream state. When we're in a holding pattern, we don't have to hold onto the dream for real. Because if we do, there's a chance it may slip, or drop or break. It's safer to keep sleeping on it.

As much as Charlie wants to find the winning ticket, his hold on the dream goes only as far as opening two Wonka Bars. He's playing it safe. Veruka, for all her faults, takes the initiative, puts a white-knuckle grip on her dream and demands that her father's employees shell 19,000 Wonka Bars an hour!

Charlie's "safe thinking" is revealed when he stops by his mother's work, asks if he can walk her home, and announces the third ticket was found. When his mother responds by wondering aloud who the lucky two remaining will be, Charlie says with defeat, "Well, in case you're wondering if it will be me, it won't be. Just in case you're wondering, you can count me out."

"You can count me out." Charlie's emotion is understandable, isn't it? Haven't we all, to some degree, been conditioned to accept the advice to not get our hopes up? "It's not fair to raise his hopes," Mrs. Bucket says aloud as Charlie cautiously opens a Wonka Bar. Playing it safe may seem like self-preservation, but practically speaking, it's self defeat. Therefore, how do we hold on tight to our dreams and their achievement, despite the fear or losing our grip, and the dream, altogether?

## Opposites Don't Attract

The answer may lie in rejecting the romantic notion that "opposites attract." Something called the law of attraction has been written about and practiced for centuries. It holds that we inevitably attract into our lives the people and circumstances that harmonize with our dominant thoughts.

I know, this seems like self-help happy talk. There have been countless books and articles written about this idea. And who among us hasn't thought about what we want to have, and do and be and yet remain largely in the same place. I suspect, though, that we can all find examples—perhaps not monumentally life-altering ones—where this has happened, where we internalized a desire and pursued it long enough to bring it into reality.

*Pursued it long enough.* If there's any "secret" to this law, that's it. Charlie had desire—he wished for a golden ticket and dwelled on that wish continuously. That's building castles in the air, the dreaming part. The foundation building is actual physical activity, no different from building a house. It's bringing the "meaning to do" (for example, blueprints) into reality (a house) with action (labor and materials). It's getting started, however modest that start may be, and building momentum. Turning to our song, it's risking rejection to start a relationship with a new someone so you don't just live in a dream world.

## 176,249,054 to 1

One hundred seventy-six million, two hundred forty-nine thousand, fifty-four. To one. Phew! These were the odds of winning a recent Mega Millions jackpot. What were anyone's chance of winning? Virtually zero, but some "lucky person" claimed the prize. Charlie was "lucky" in finding the last golden ticket. But who wants to play in life's lottery with those odds? "A dollar and a dream" is a catchy tagline, but you're better off investing a dollar in your dream and pursuing it with a plan, with purpose and persistence.

We may have goals that seem as impossible to reach as winning a 176-million-to-one Mega Millions lottery. But whereas dreaming is the staying point in a lottery, it's only the starting point when we decide to pursue our dreams and create better odds for reaching them. That's when we "get out of bed" and get going, which we'll talk about in the next chapter. C'mon!

### morsels to munch on

◈ Wake up! Dreaming is the starting point, not the staying point.

◈ Don't break the law—of attraction (but don't count on it entirely).

◈ A dollar and a dream is not a good plan to invest in.

# Lesson Three

## Get Out of Bed!

*Tomorrow is often the busiest day of the week.*
—Spanish proverb

It's really a bizarre scene. Charlie's two sets of grandparents, bedridden for the last 20 years, their "bedroom" situated in the middle of the Buckets' cramped living room. Grandpa Joe, Grandma Josephine, Grandpa George and Grandma Georgina. They seemed to have accepted their "fate." They sleep most of the day, watch TV and wait to be served a bowl of cabbage water for dinner.

They live what Henry David Thoreau called "lives of quiet desperation." Whatever dreams they had as children and as adults died long ago. By their own choosing. What a waste.

## Today *Is* Tomorrow

It's what Grandpa Joe has said for years. As soon as he gets his strength back. Tomorrow, he'll do it. Tomorrow he'll get out of bed. And tomorrow comes, and tomorrow goes. Soon, others around him don't put any stock into his declaration. "Dad, in all the years you've been saying you're going to get out of that bed, I've yet to see you set one foot on the floor" said Charlie's mother. To which he replied, "Well... maybe if the floor wasn't so cold."

Guess what—there will always be a cold floor, if that's all you choose to see. There is a world of possibilities beyond the cold floor—yes, there will be some discomfort, but the floor won't always stay cold when you start walking on it.

## Time to Make the Donuts

He was someone who did get out of bed—every morning, at 3:00 a.m., but had the weight of the world on his shoulders as he uttered what would become an iconic catchphrase: "Time to make the donuts, time to make the donuts." America fell in love with Fred the Baker of Dunkin Donuts commercial fame in the 1980s, probably because it was so easy to relate to his daily, humdrum, "responsible" routine. You may fall into a similar pattern, and find yourself rushing through the equivalent of making the donuts, just to get it done, to be over with. "I made the donuts" Fred would dryly say as he returned home, apparently having had an entirely unsatisfying day.

Maybe it's the daily checklist, your child's homework or school project, running on errands, making the bed, walking the dog or some other "have to do it" activity that you rush to get through. But as soon as it's done, there will be something else, and something else again.

It's true, we won't accomplish anything if we don't get out of our physical and metaphorical bed. But going through the motions feels like busywork, like filling out worksheets for a substitute teacher. We're not getting anything out of it.

It could appear that Mrs. Bucket, Charlie's mom, lives a humdrum, unfulfilling, "just making the donuts" life. Granted, hers is not an easy one. Widowed, she cares for Charlie and all four grandparents, cleans the home, works in a laundry and doesn't have any time for herself. Yet she never complains; she appreciates the little things and remains optimistic about the future.

When Charlie brings home a loaf of bread for dinner, she remarks, "We'll have a real banquet." She invites him to "pull up a pile of clothes and sit down" when he stops by the laundry and, sensing he's down, encourages him. "Charlie, you'll get your chance. One day, things will change." She's happy simply being around her son and sings, "His grin has always been my sunshine."

The "Fred the Bakers" of the world may find inspiration in the Mrs. Buckets around them. The bakers have probably stopped appreciating the wonderful smell of freshly baked donuts—theirs for the taking every morning. The equivalent of freshly baked donuts is around us more than we realize. If you've allowed yourself to be weighed down with the "time to make the donuts" stuff, it's never too late to wake up and smell their aroma.

## I'll Gladly Pay You Tuesday for a Hamburger Today

A catchphrase made famous by the character Wimpy from the Popeye comic strip and cartoons, this expression is now commonly used to illustrate undesirable behaviors like being lazy, slothful and undisciplined. Interestingly, there may be some helpful "get out of bed" psychology here.

In a study published in the journal *Appetite* (stay with me!), the authors advance the "compensatory beliefs model" and conclude that when faced with temptation, people form intentions to compensate behaviorally for indulgence. Thus, the dieter faces the temptation of choosing to eat something delicious but high in calories or a less delicious alternative, but one that adheres to the goal of losing weight. The conflict is resolved by eating the high-caloric food—but having the mental intention to "make up for it" later (skip a meal, eat less, exercise, etc.).

However, many dieters do not regularly follow through on these compensatory intentions, just like Wimpy never gets around to paying for the burgers and Grandpa Joe never gets out of bed. Whatever the desired behavior was resolved to be starts to fade away, and eventually, so does the goal. The solution is to form the habit of paying the price today. I guarantee, when you pay the price today, you won't suffer from buyer's remorse!

## Yes, Burn Your Bridges

Hmmm. Burn our bridges? Doesn't that advice fly in the face of contemporary wisdom? Maybe, but not when it comes to paying the price today. Back to Lesson Two and the gentleman who is dreaming his life away. He claims he can make the object of his desire "mine," "anytime night or day." So, when anytime arrives, and he is faced with the choice of approaching her or not, the conflict is resolved by passing up on it this time, but mentally intending to do it next time. And as we know, he goes back to dreaming his life away. So, good intentions, bad execution!

How does one effectively burn the bridge of the intentional "next time"? It helps to create optimal conditions that make it more likely the intentions will materialize. For example, we intend to get up early and exercise for 30 minutes before getting ready for work. Setting the alarm clock for 5:30 a.m. versus 6:00 a.m. creates that condition. But, if you leave the snooze feature on, you may go through three or four snooze cycles and miss the 30-minute window.

If you are really committed to getting up early to exercise, move the alarm clock from the nightstand to a spot on the other side of the room where you will be forced to physically get up to turn it off. Is it possible you will simply drag yourself back to bed? Yes, but now that you are up, the likelihood that you will follow through on your intention is greatly increased.

When it comes to dieting, say no at the supermarket to the high-caloric, low-nutritional "food stuff" so you don't have to fight saying no at home during a vulnerable moment. Snack machines at work calling out your name every time you walk by? Then leave your cash and coins in the car, way out in the parking lot, so you don't have the means of selecting F5 to drop a bag of chips out of the slot and into your eager hands.

## Desperately Seeking Dissatisfaction

Probably not a personal ad one would place. "Looking for someone who enjoys candlelit dinners, walks on the beach, and cuddling by the fire and who is dissatisfied with their life, like I am." Beyond the general cheesiness of such an ad, who would respond to that?

Fortunately, there can be an upside to dissatisfaction. It signals we are not pleased, not content, with our current state or condition. It's this internal dissatisfaction that can act as the impetus to get out of bed. When Charlie cried out, "I'm fed up with cabbage water. It's not enough!" he was sufficiently dissatisfied to do something about it.

I'm a big fan of the classic self-help authors like W. Clement Stone, who, in his autobiography, *The Success System That Never Fails,* coined the term inspirational dissatisfaction. Although Stone wore a bow tie, he was no-bow-tie academic, adrift in theory. Born into a poor and disadvantaged situation, he eventually built a multimillion dollar insurance company from a $100 investment. His resilience was sustained by his unwavering belief that if there's something in our lives we don't like, a condition we can't bear, we must be the change agents. Nobody else is going to change it for us. Nobody else is coming to the rescue.

## If It Wasn't For...

It's difficult to get out of bed if you have chosen an "if it wasn't for" mindset. If it wasn't for my job, my education, my childhood, my spouse, my kids, my parents, my boss, my (fill in the blank), then my life would be what I want it to be, what I dreamed it would be.

If it wasn't for. If it wasn't for. If it wasn't for. If anyone was "entitled" to an attitude of "if it wasn't for," it was Charlie's mother—a poor widow raising a son and taking care of four bedridden seniors, all by herself. But she chose not to adopt that attitude. So we must be wary of victim language like "if it wasn't for" because it leads us down an emotional one-way, dead end street. A place where you won't be able to go left, or right, to get out of there. You'll be boxed in, stuck in a dark alley, seemingly forever. What can you do?

Don't go down the emotional dark alley. "Oh, that's real helpful," you're thinking. "I know that!" Okay, then, why are you there? You're driving the car, right? That's what people forget, they are driving the car. You are only in the passenger seat when you are passive, and allow yourself not to be in control of things that are controllable. Feeling like you are in control of your life is the starting point to taking control of your life. Do you prefer to be the one holding the remote control when watching TV? Of course you do. And it's the same with our lives.

In psychology, a concept called the Theory of Control, developed by Julian Rotter in the1950s, refers to how people interpret the underlying causes of events in their lives. People can be externally oriented, where luck, fate or external influences are held responsible for everything that happens to them. Or, they can be just the opposite and internally oriented, where their mantra is "If it's to be, it's entirely up to me."

Although an extreme of either is not ideal, it is generally agreed that an internal locus of control is more desirable than an external one. That's because it is psychologically healthier (not to mention practically healthier) to believe one can influence or control things that are controllable.

A good barometer to gauge your sense of control is to listen to your language. Is it holding-the-remote-control kind of language, or is it couch-potato, subject-to-the-whims-of-others language? For example, do you say "I choose to be this way," or do you say "Well, that's just the way I am." "I can" versus "I can't." "I want to" or "I have to." It may seem overly simplistic, but give the remote-control-in-your-hand language a try. Because as opposed to saying "I'm stuck in this one-way, dead-end alley," you may find yourself saying, "I may not be able to make a right or a left, but

I can choose to go in reverse or make a u-turn and get of here. I'll find the way."

## What's Your "Why"?

A favorite saying of my grandmother was "Why do you do like you do do?" As a kid, I liked it because it sounded funny, but I didn't give much thought to it at the time. Grandma was on to something though. Because the "why" can be our friend or an enemy. It can help us or hurt us. And one's "why" is always self-selected. Always. Grandpa Joe has his why when Charlie invites him to the chocolate factory. Yes, he had been bedridden for the past 20 years and hadn't stood up in all that time (his choice); but when Charlie asked if he would come on the chocolate factory tour, something clicked—and Grandpa Joe made a decision, right then, to get out of bed, to take action, to move forward. Did he fall down after getting up? Yes. Did he need some help from Charlie to get his balance? Yes. But with concentration and effort, he was soon singing and dancing all around the house.

What's your "why"? Is it having a fulfilling family life, watching your kids grow up, becoming financially independent or enjoying better relationships? If your "why" is big enough, the "how" will take care of itself. And, don't be embarrassed to ask for some help or for a shoulder to lean until you've got your footing.

So, what's your "why"? You probably know the answer. Now, get out of bed and get to it!

## morsels to munch on

◈ Throw off the covers of fear and get out of bed!

◈ Remember, today *is* tomorrow.

◈ Dissatisfied? Good! Now be inspirationally dissatisfied.

◈ Pay the price today for what you want, and you'll never suffer from buyer's remorse.

# Lesson Four

## If at First You Don't Succeed, Buy Another Chocolate Bar

*I haven't failed. I've just found 10,000 ways that won't work.*

—Thomas Edison

The last golden ticket had been found. Charlie's dream is shattered, and he tries to find solace in buying himself some chocolate at Bill's Candy Shop. He devours some candy, and could have bought himself more, but decides to use his last few cents to buy Grandpa Joe a Wonka Bar.

As he walks out of the shop, the news breaks: The last golden ticket found was determined to be a fraud. There was still one left—and Charlie had just bought a Wonka Bar for his grandpa. Maybe, just maybe. He slowly unwraps the bar and voila! There it is, the last golden ticket!

## Three Strikes and You're In

The winning ticket had been in the third chocolate bar Charlie opened. He earlier failed in finding one, but an unexpected chance opened up, and he was in a position to take advantage of it. We should all embrace the maxim, "If at first you don't succeed, try, try again." Failing is in the act, not in the person. One could argue that Thomas Edison, the most prolific inventor in history, was also the greatest failure by virtue of how often his experiments failed. That's the key insight—how often his *experiments* failed, not him. He held 1,093 patents! If that's failure, sign me up!

If 10,000 attempts at trying to accomplish something seems a bit daunting (and I'm with you, it does!) why not commit to at least three attempts? It's reasonable and palpable. There's something hopeful in the expression, "third time's the charm." The game of baseball allows us to "fail" with three strikes before we're out. (But when the next inning roles around, we're up again!) More important than the number of attempts is how our mindset to approaching challenges and opportunities changes for the better when we won't let temporary defeat knock us off our two feet for good.

## Metaphor of the Tangled Necklace

A tiny strand of gold to the left, a tiny strand of gold to the right, and in the middle, a gold cluster twisted up like a pretzel. That's what it looked like in the palm of my daughter's hand as she stood in front of me, arm extended, and asked, "Dad, can you untangle this?" Untangling a necklace is a pretty good metaphor for "try, try again." Ideally, it's best to have "the best laid plans of mice and men" before moving forward, but sometimes, you just have to get started, not knowing exactly what may work, but with a goal in sight—in this case, returning the necklace to its original, untangled state. Thus, you loosen up this little section, pull an end through that little opening and... you strike out this time as it becomes more tangled! So, you start over again in a different way, on a different little piece of the chain, pulling here, loosening there, and all of a sudden the necklace seems to unravel itself, and the problem is resolved.

Not a bad vignette to remember the next time your favorite piece of jewelry is tangled, but more importantly, when the next challenge is in front of you. Get started, do this, stop that, remain cool and keep trying, all the while remembering what the result should be. Eventually, you'll find the right chocolate bar.

## Trivial Pursuit

It's a board game that peaked in popularity in the '80s and is still sold today. The player who answers the most questions about general knowledge and popular culture wins. Here, knowing a little bit about a lot of things is an advantage. But when we are pursuing a goal—something not trivial—it helps to have a more focused, single-mindedness of purpose.

Motivational speaker Zig Ziglar suggests we start reaching our goals when we "stop being a wandering generality and start becoming a meaningful specific." Grandpa Joe displayed single-mindedness or what Napoleon Hill referred to as "definiteness of purpose" when he decided to get out of bed after 20 years. Think about it—it becomes increasingly difficult to stay motivated to "try, try again" when we are trying too many things.

## Magnify the Problem

Increasing our odds of success requires increasing the intensity our focus. Think about the potential of a magnifying glass on a sunny day. If the glass is held steady, at the correct angle, long enough, the sun's rays ignite the timber below. However, if the magnifying glass is held briefly but then put down, or the correct angle of the lens is not kept consistent, the timber won't ignite. It may not even get warm. The investment in time may be identical in both scenarios, but the one where concentrated effort has been applied yields the best return.

Charlie invested time in thinking about the big win, but didn't apply any real effort beyond opening a couple of Wonka Bars.

## Talk to Me

To persist, we need to stay motivated. We may not have someone giving a pep talk to us every day, but we are talking to ourselves all day long. Some thoughts are involuntary, but most we choose to initiate, like in any conversation. Our thoughts can fuel us or fatigue us. (I can't even imagine what the bedridden grandparents thought about all day.)

This begs the question: What exactly are we thinking about most of the day? Is the internal dialogue running in our heads helping us pursue our dreams and taking us toward our desires—or away from them? If you were not you, but you could eavesdrop on the conversation you're having with yourself, would you want to join in? Would it be uplifting? If not, why not? Would accepting the idea of our thoughts as fuel motivate you to go for the "higher octane" more often?

## You Can't Do Anything
## You Put Your Mind To

*Can't,* in case you missed it. You can't do anything you put your mind to. (I know what you must be thinking, based on the last point, but keep reading!) I just want to be realistic—and I'm the glass-is-half-full kind of person. It's not an accident there are so few brain surgeons in the country. Most of us simply don't have the brain power to do it. Or the height and skills to play center in the NBA. But, there are lots of things we can do that brain surgeons and professional basketball players cannot. And here's the point—you can do anything you put your mind to when you play to your natural strengths and abilities, coupled with a burning desire to accomplish whatever goal you've set. That's the kind of "high octane," uplifting talk you want running through your head.

Playing to natural strengths and abilities doesn't imply not being challenged. Just ask the remarkably talented ballerina student, head and shoulders above everyone in her class, who tries out for the New York City Ballet. Despite how good she is going in, everyone on stage is better. But because she has some natural gifts, the right kind of "raw material" to be a principal dancer, she has a shot. But it's going to take thousands of hours of practice, pain and perseverance in the studio to get to the stage. "I dance on blistered feet," the accomplished ballerina poet once wrote.

Here's another way of looking at this. An apple is a delicious fruit. But if I want some delicious apple juice, I can't just stick a straw into it and suck. The apple has to go through a transformation to become juice, through a process called pressing. Only an apple will produce apple juice. An orange cannot, even if it goes through a similar process. But only oranges can make orange juice. What I'm getting at is there are genetic limitations to our aspirations. But don't despair! That means there are genetic advantages too. Thus, the more we play to our natural strengths and abilities in the pursuit of our goals, despite the inevitable ups, downs and challenges, the more we'll pick ourselves up, dust ourselves off, stay motivated and get back at it.

## Celebrate the Small Stuff

The fuel of "try, try again" is recognizing and celebrating the incremental steps and small wins. Don't wait until the journey is complete, or the tank may run dry along the way. When Charlie brought home a freshly baked loaf of bread, his mother remarked, "We'll have a banquet." That's appreciating a small win, and it can provide motivation for bigger wins.

It's important to make the milestone reachable. For example, the thought of losing 25 pounds is overwhelming and not motivating if all you see is a big 25 in front of you. But if you commit to losing just ½ pound a week, in one year, you've done it. And doesn't next year always come around quickly? How often do you say, "I can't believe it's [fill in the holiday] already." Ten minutes of exercise a day (can you do five minutes in the a.m. and five in the p.m.?) and passing up the seconds on dessert (one cookie instead of two) will probably get you there. Even if you only reach 70% of your goal (a grade of C), you've lost 18 pounds! Little steps can lead to great destinations, but the little step needs to be taken and celebrated—and taken and celebrated again and again.

## If You Aren't Dead Yet,
## There's Still Hope

When he learned the "last" Wonka Bar was found, Grandpa Joe, frustrated and sensitive to Charlie's disappointment, remarked, "A little boy's got to have something in this world to hope for. What's he got to hope for now?" Seems a bit trivial, putting so much importance on a contest, but to Charlie, not finding a golden ticket was devastating. Still, one must remain hopeful. The sun will rise tomorrow; and if for some reason it doesn't, we're all in the same boat! Hang on to hope, even if that's all you have left. But continue to "buy another chocolate bar" and move forward, if only with baby steps, and things will get better. You'll see.

## morsels to munch on

◈ Failure is only in the act, never in the person.

◈ Be a meaningful specific versus a wandering generality!

◈ Eavesdrop on your own internal dialogue— what are you saying?

◈ Play to your natural strengths, talents and abilities. You will stay motivated—and chalk up more wins than losses.

# Lesson Five

## The Good Can Be Bad and Ugly

*So of cheerfulness, or a good temper, the more it is spent,*
*the more it remains.*
—Ralph Waldo Emerson

Recall Wonka's tirade when he was yelling at Charlie and Grandpa Joe. "You stole fizzy lifting drinks. You bumped into the ceiling which now has to be washed and sterilized, so you get nothing! You lose! Good day, Sir!" By all accounts, Charlie and his Grandpa were good people—honest, good natured, considerate, polite—and not at all like the other selfish children who were on the tour. They did not see themselves "stealing" fizzy lifting drink or acting out of line, but they were caught up in the moment, threw caution to the wind and behaved in a way inconsistent with their character. Simply put, they were wrong.

## To Be or Not to Be

That really is the question. Who do we want to be and who do we want not to be? Want or want not, the choice is ours, always. And choice forms habit—from good choices flow good habits and from bad choices, bad habits. If given a choice, we would all embrace good habits versus bad ones. Well, it is a choice, isn't it? And like decisions, there are consequences to habits. If you form the habit of eating properly and exercising regularly, it won't be an accident that you're fit and healthy. Conversely, if a diet is largely hamburgers, Heinekens and Häagen Dazs, being fit and healthy? Not so much!

The importance of habits as the building blocks of a great life is wonderfully captured in the following quote, the gift of an unknown author: "Sow an act, and you reap a habit. Sow a habit and you reap a character. Sow a character, and you reap a destiny."

In behaving a certain way, just like in performing a task over and over again, we reach a point of autopilot. This repetition programs our internal navigation system, like a car's GPS, to take us to our distinct, yet predictable way of acting, of thinking, of doing. We "recalculate" as needed and don't have to think about getting to our desired "behavioral destination" because it has become second nature. If we've programmed the destination to be a good person—honest, reasonable, respectful, intelligent and mature—that's how we'll behave, most of the time.

Occasionally, a GPS malfunctions, and so will we. But make this the exception, not the rule. In sneaking away during the tour, Charlie and Grandpa Joe went off course from how they routinely behaved. We've all done the same, more times than we'd like to admit. And sometimes, our behavior really can be "bad and ugly." It may happen while arguing with our spouse or significant other, dealing with colleagues at work, gossiping with friends or not behaving like the adult in front of our children. We should regret it, because it's a departure from our "normal."

But remember, the human condition that permits us to fall from grace is the same one that can bounce us back as well. Liberate yourself from the "bad and ugly" moments in life by being deliberate in who you choose to be and how you choose to behave. When we choose to define ourselves, circumstances can't choose for us.

## We Have a Lot of Chemistry

One more thought on "to be or not to be." It is impossible for one to be in a state of X while simultaneously not being in a state of X. In junior high chemistry, we learned that water exists in a solid, liquid or gaseous state but cannot exist as a solid (ice cube) and gas (steam) or any combination of the three at exactly the same time. Chemically speaking, water will always be defined as $H_2O$, regardless of its state of matter. We are similar in that we remain "us" despite the state of our behavior at a given time, like when Charlie violated the rules of Wonka's chocolate factory. We should, however, choose our ideal state to be in, because when we do not, by default, we'll be acting in another *manner* altogether, and one probably not so ideal.

## A Pillow Out of Place

Talking about "bad and ugly," has a pillow out of place ever thrown you into a bad and ugly state? I'm referring to those throw pillows on the sofa that you sometimes find aren't fluffed the way you left them. Think of a pillow out of place as a metaphor for the endless little things we allow to annoy us and potentially set us off. If we put the pillows back ourselves, it would take all of three seconds. But seeking out the responsible party to "express" our frustration to will take a lot longer and may escalate into something totally unrelated to the pillows. And you'll still probably end up fixing them yourself.

"Bad and ugly" reacting overpowers the good person you are. There may seem to be some justification for the behavior, but it won't solve the root cause behind it. That's another conversation.

Aristotle spoke of the golden mean, the desirable middle between two extremes. Confucius called it the doctrine of the mean; Buddha called it the middle way. It's all about balance. If there's a house rule nobody seems to be following except you, it needs to be addressed. But ensure it's done in the context of all the house rules' being carried out just fine.

Next time, just fluff!

## Have It Your Way, Have It Your Way

The "Have It Your Way" Burger King campaign first launched in the '70s. A memorable line from the jingle was "Hold the pickles, hold the lettuce, special orders won't upset us, all we ask is that you let us serve it your way."

Having it our way is very satisfying. We like our way and mostly think our way is better than other ways (just look at Veruka Salt!) Our way keeps us feeling in control, and feeling good.

In real life, though, we generally don't have happy, smiling people ready to satisfy our every desire like in the commercial. So we get to our way by doing everything ourselves, which can be frustrating and may lead to a meltdown into "bad and ugly" because we're already drained, emotionally and physically. But others around us are willing to help out—so let them, but do so knowing (and accepting cheerfully) that that their way of doing things may be different from your way.

## The Publishers Clearing House
## Light of Truth

Does being at your "wits' end" occur with too much regularity? Difficult to see more than five minutes ahead of the present situation? Saying things to your family like, "You think I like being this way, yelling all the time?" Or, "I can't help it if I'm angry!" Has the morning scene become something you'd rather not be seen in? Let's suppose that you didn't sleep well, you're frustrated with your spouse over last night's unfinished argument and the kids are complaining about the breakfast you've served them. You're at your wits' end, and have let everybody know it with a few choice words. You feel you have lost control of your life.

Then the doorbell rings. Outside is a van, camera crews and someone with a microphone. Congratulations—you have just won $1,000,000 in the Publishers Clearing House Sweepstakes and are handed the famous, oversized check. In seconds a bad attitude becomes a glad attitude, out of control becomes in control and the mantra of "I don't have a life" is now "I have *the* life."

A positive transformation has occurred, literally in seconds. Why shouldn't it? You're a millionaire! But, what if it wasn't true? Somebody was playing a joke. You had been "punked." Until Ashton Kucher (or an Ed McMahon lookalike) appeared at the door, your brain had processed the situation as real. You decided at that very moment how to feel. Granted, $1,000,000 cash will make most of us feel pretty good (just like discovering a golden ticket), but the money itself is neutral. You decided that the money was desirable, and your brain accepted that input. You chose how to feel.

Remember, nothing has changed since the doorbell rang. You still hadn't slept well, the unfinished argument with your spouse was left unfinished and the kids still don't appreciate the breakfast you made. But now life is great! Until we learn it is not true. Now life stinks again.

When you're feeling that slow simmer of frustration, annoyance and discontent, it doesn't have to reach the boiling point. There are probably some very real "Publisher's Clearing House moments" in your life, knocking outside. Decide right now that it's time to open the door, and yourself, to them.

## Is This a Wise Decision?

You're driving on the highway and see the traffic signal ahead. It's green, but as you approach, the light turns yellow. Do you typically speed up or slow down? Most of us have probably raced past more of these intersections than we would like to admit. Not the best course of action, as yellow's purpose is to slow us down, to make sure that the road ahead is safe. Traffic signals have conditioned us to go on green and stop on red. No one thinks about what to do on red and green. But yellow, that's a little different. When we choose to speed through the intersection, there's a moment of pause. Should I or shouldn't I?

Even if we behave largely by following the green and red signals in our lives, there is still a strong need for a yellow signal, to slow us down, to pause and possibly help prevent our going to that "bad and ugly" place.

Therefore, we need to create our life's own yellow signal. Asking the question, "Is this a wise decision?" can act as the cautionary yellow light we need. If we develop the habit of asking that question, over and over again, answering it will become as secondary to us as what we do at a traffic light when the signal is red or green. If Charlie and Grandpa Joe had slowed momentarily at their personal yellow light and asked, "Is this a wise decision?" chances are they would have immediately dismissed the idea of drinking fizzy lifting drink because it was not an act consistent with who they were.

Stop at the reds, go at the greens, pause at the yellows, ask the "wise" question and more times than not, you'll drive right past "bad and ugly" and arrive at your desired, ideal behavioral destination.

## morsels to munch on

◈ Who do you want "to be or not to be"? That is the question.

◈ Develop the habit of asking yourself, "Is this a wise decision?"

◈ Open your emotional and mental door to life's good things knocking at it.

# Lesson Six

## Revenge Is Never Sweet

*Revenge has no more quenching effect on emotions than salt water has on thirst.*

—Walter Weckler

Mr. Beauregarde, seeing his daughter blow up like a giant blueberry, told Wonka that he would break him and threatened, "I'll get even with you for this, Wonka, if it's the last thing I ever do." Grandpa Joe was angry at Wonka for not granting Charlie the lifetime supply of chocolate and was ready to ruin him by giving Slugworth, Wonka's archenemy, the coveted everlasting gobstopper.

Why are we so quick to seek revenge? Is it simply our nature? Can we rise above it? Ernst Fehr, director of the Institute of Empirical Research in Economics at the University of Zurich in Switzerland, conducted a brain imaging study that suggests that we feel satisfaction when we punish others for their bad behavior. Too often, I'm afraid, the bad behavior we ascribe to others is rooted in feeling personally offended by something they said or did, so we think we'll feel better if we "get back" at them. In wanting to punish Wonka for his perceived injustice, Beauregarde and Grandpa Joe's threats followed Fehr's theory. They blamed Wonka for the problems they caused and self-ignited the spark of revenge.

## The Economics of Revenge

Economics is about how people make choices. The first principle in economics is that we live in a world of scarcity and the second, that we have unlimited wants and desires. The third principle follows that we have to make choices. A classic economic example is the guns-and-butter model, where a nation chooses between two options when spending its finite resources. It can buy guns (defense,) butter (goods) or a combination of both. Spending more on one leaves less to invest in the other. What's most important? That's up to the individual nation.

Similarly, we choose how we spend our finite resources. As human beings, a finite resource is our energy. There's only so much to spend physically and mentally before we're "out." When it's invested in "wanting to get even-ism" like we saw in Beauregarde and Grandpa Joe's behavior, that's energy, that's emotion, that won't go toward positive pursuits. It's been used up.

In short, any investment of energy or emotion into revenge is a bad bet. Eventually, we'll be broke. Broken families, broken friendships, broken spirits.

And it doesn't have to be a flashpoint. A desire for revenge can simply start with the slow simmer of a grudge over some "offense" by someone—but then heat up into a troubled relationship and boil over to an all-consuming pursuit of perverted personal justice that ends in tragedy and appears on the front page of the newspaper.

## Wisdom of a Chinese Gardener

"The first year they sleep. The second year they creep. The third year they leap!" This is how the gardener described Moso, the Chinese bamboo plant that shows no visible growth above the surface for years but then suddenly explodes, growing 75 feet or more in five years (up to 2½ feet per day!) How is this possible? Because for years, the plant developed miles of roots beneath the surface, getting ready.

When the story of the Moso bamboo tree, or "Lesson of the Moso" is used for motivational purposes, the point is that if you lay the groundwork for your success—working hard, preparing, studying, saving, etc.—you may not see signs of progress for some time. But then suddenly, your hard work starts to pay off, sometimes in a big way. I agree with the analogy. I believe there is a corollary as well, a "dark side" of the lesson. That is, if you allow the roots of resentment, grudges and "get even-ism" to grow inside of you, beneath the surface, they eventually will surface—and could explode into a towering tree of revenge.

## Road Outrageous

We floor the accelerator, move quickly into the fast lane, throw caution to the wind and don't check our blind spot (Who has time? This is really important!), race past the guy who just cut us off, position ourselves just a little past his car and then steer hard right to get in front of him, braking quickly, hopefully making him slam on his brakes and in the process "teaching him a lesson." Boy, that felt good… for about three seconds. This is what they call road rage, but perhaps it should be coined road revenge. Because it's all about getting back at the "offender."

I'm not a fan of creating a diagnosis for every behavior under the sun. It leaves wiggle room for excuses, as if the condition of "road rage" compels someone to act like a maniac in their car versus choosing to act like a maniac in their car. We become indignant beyond belief because of a chance occurrence with a rude, careless and anonymous driver who we will never see again for the rest of our lives. Yet, it's payback time, Baby!

I'll admit, I "suffered" from a few instances of road rage in my early 20s. Hmm. Do you see how framing it up like that absolves me of my behavior? No, I didn't suffer from anything, I chose to act like a fool! Anyway, an older, wiser driver cured me one afternoon. He accidently cut me off, so of course, I indignantly sped ahead of him, cut in front and immediately slammed on the brakes. Then, I really showed him who's who when I pointed and shook my index finger at him in the rear view mirror. He sees it, and returns some sort of gesture. This goes on for a couple of minutes until he raises a clenched fist and makes a "lets fight" signal, inviting me to pull into the parking lot on the right. Remember, *he's behind me.* I take him up on his challenge and righteously pull off the highway into the parking lot. And what does my dueling road-rage partner do? He just keeps driving on the highway, right past me! Yeah, I taught him a lesson!

There's an expression that says when a person with experience meets a person with money, the person with the experience ends up with the money and the person with the money ends up with the experience (Mr. Salt and his daughter come to mind.)

We may not have exchanged money that day, but I definitely ended up with the experience. Thankfully, it was a good experience about the futility of revenge, and one that has probably saved me some traffic tickets too!

## morsels to munch on

◈ Let go of the grudge.

◈ Get rid of "get even" thinking—immediately.

◈ There is no upside to revenge. None.

# Lesson Seven

## The Good Humor Man or Woman

*Like a welcome summer rain, humor may suddenly*
*cleanse and cool the earth, the air and you.*

—Langston Hughes

It's called "the best medicine" by *Reader's Digest*. We have a "funny bone" and love watching a good comedy. We are drawn to humor like a moth to a flame.

Throughout the movie, we witness Wonka defusing tense situations and calming his guests with his quick wit and dry sense of humor. When Mr. Salt exclaims, "I doubt any of us will get out of here alive," Wonka, retorts bizarrely, "Oh, you should never, never doubt what nobody is sure about." When Augustus is stuck in the pipe, his mother cries out, "He's gone! He'll be made into marshmallows in five seconds!" Wonka snaps back. "Impossible, my dear lady. That's absurd! Unthinkable!" "Why?" she asks. "Because that pipe doesn't go into the marshmallow room; it goes into the fudge room." After Wonka asks the children to sign the contract for entrance into the factory, Mrs. Teavee says, "I assume there's an accident indemnity clause," to which Wonka replies, only half jokingly, "Never between friends."

These silly comebacks are sprinkled throughout the movie, and it's his demeanor and delivery that make them so effective. Humor disarms. It would be near impossible to stay angry at Wonka for any length of time.

## But I'm Not Funny

That's okay. But are you fun, or are you glum? You may not make it as a standup comedian (and probably wouldn't want to today, for what passes as humor in many comedy clubs), but can you laugh at yourself?

When we don't take ourselves too seriously (need I remind you of the whimsical fellow in the purple hat and coat?), we'll be open to the funny things around us at home or work. You don't need to possess the comic genius of a Jay Leno either. There is a lot of material in all those "do-overs" we wish we could have. "Some-day, we'll all laugh about this," we say. Well, what about laughing about it now? That's a fun person… maybe not the last comic standing, but a stand-out person others like and want to be around.

## Say Cheese!

It's difficult to be fun or of good cheer without a smile! The *Wall Street Journal* reported that the physical act of smiling can make people feel better. "Research shows that when people say the long "e" sound, which is easier to sound with a smile, they feel more positive emotion compared to when they say the German word "fur," which requires on to pucker one's lips, simulating a negative emotional expression." It goes on to report that brain temperatures vary according to which expression one is making, reflecting either a positive or negative mood state.

Even if you don't feel like smiling, do it anyway. You may be surprised how you can "trick" yourself into genuinely feeling better. And smiling is one of the few things that the more you give it away, the more it comes back to you. Isn't it hard not to smile back when someone flashes you a smile? Dale Carnegie wrote of smiling in his classic book, *How to Win Friends and Influence People,* that smiling "costs nothing, but creates much. It enriches those who receive, without impoverishing those who give. It happens in a flash and the memory of it sometimes lasts forever." Now, that's a win-win you can have every day!

## Laughter Is Serious Business

It's pretty serious when something has an effect on our health. Laughter has an effect—a positive one that reduces the level of stress hormones like cortisol, epinephrine, dopamine and growth hormone, all contributors to stress. Stress is understandable but inward focused, and controllable. When you are under stress, it's hard to see five minutes in front of you.

Think about times when you've been arguing with someone and something unexpectedly funny is said—what happens? For a brief moment, there's a smile, a laugh and the intensity of the situation diminishes. Mrs. Gloop is understandably frantic when young Augustus falls into the river. "He can't swim!" she cries, to which Wonka replies, "There's no better time to learn."

## If Attitude Were Contagious, Would You Want to Catch Yours?

I saw that posted on a church sign. You've probably seen them, catchy little messages posted on a church's marquee that are sometimes funny, deep, practical or unexpected, but usually provoke a "hmm, how true" from the passerby. If you were driving by that sign, how would you answer the question, "If attitude were contagious, would you want to catch yours?" Thought provoking, isn't it?

This is when you need to apply what former General Electric CEO Jack Welch called "the reality principle." In dealing with a business issue, he always asked his management team, "What's the reality here?" The idea is to be brutally honest about a situation. What's the reality of your attitude? If an anonymous poll was taken among your circle of family, friends and co-workers, asking about the kind of attitude and temperament you typically display, what would the results be?

If yours is genuinely positive and uplifting like Wonka's, not only is that a plus for you and your state of mind, it's a plus for those around you. But maybe your attitude is somewhat unpredictable, like Veruka's—sometimes positive, sometimes negative; sometimes up, sometimes down—like a roller coaster. That's because we allow circumstances to influence how we feel, rather than choosing for ourselves.

Years ago, I read Holocaust survivor Victor Frankl's book, *Man's Search for Meaning,* and was struck by his observation than even in a depraved and dehumanized situation like a concentration camp, the ability to choose how one would feel and think and be could not be taken away.

Okay, Victor Frankl is pretty serious stuff, and this is supposed to be the lighthearted chapter! Just remember, being good humored isn't necessarily being the one who is funny; it's about being someone who can be fun and appreciate the funny in others. Good-humored people are serious about the important things in life, but they don't take themselves too seriously. They're people who can initiate a smile and reciprocate one back. C'mon, give it a try—Cheeeeeeeeeeeeese!

## morsels to munch on

◈ You don't have to be the funny one to have a good sense of humor.

◈ Laughter can be the best medicine to treat a difficult situation.

◈ Smiling is one of the few things that the more you give it away, the more it comes back to you.

# Lesson Eight
## Forgive and Forget... Regret

*Everyone loves the idea of forgiveness until they have something to forgive.*
—C. S. Lewis

Wonka could have remained angry and disappointed with Charlie and his Grandpa. After all, they did break the rules and stole fizzy lifting drink, which resulted in the candy maker's having to spend money to clean up their mistake. But he decided to forgive them, and by letting go of his righteous indignation, actually helped realize his own dream too. He knew that although Charlie wasn't perfect, he was the perfect person to take over the factory. Charlie's genuine remorse was proof of it. And that was enough for Wonka.

## Be Selfish... and Forgive?

Forgiving someone who has done you an injustice is challenging because the hurt doesn't magically vanish.

You still have to rise above the offense, even in the face of a sincere apology. When the offense is of a nature where you've decided to never forgive, that's when it's time to get selfish and forgive anyway. Yes, *selfish*. It's in not forgiving that you imprison yourself. You voluntarily shackle and enslave yourself to an unhealthy state of mind, way of thinking and state of being.

There's a lot of science to the medical benefits of forgiveness. There's also some good old-fashioned biblical advice in Matthew 18:18 that says, what is bound on earth, is bound in heaven and what is loosed on earth will be loosed in heaven. You don't have to be religious to benefit from that idea. Because if you don't let go of hurt and resentment while you are alive, you most certainly will take it to your grave.

## Why Wait to Wake Up at the Wake?

Or, you could take the hurt and resentment to someone else's grave. And be stuck with regret—for missed opportunities to have offered or accepted an olive branch or to have given up on being angry or hurt. All the family gatherings not attended, the grandchildren unseen, Christmas cards not mailed or displayed, time wasted on being "right." And for what? Most likely, for something not very important anyway.

If the finality of death clarifies our perspective on what's important right now, and how we should be living, what are we waiting for?

## Turnovers Aren't Just for Apples

The sooner we can forgive and forget, the better. Ever have an argument with a neighbor, one whom you've got along with splendidly, and afterwards the friendly good morning was replaced with an unfriendly good riddance? You try to avoid seeing each other, because when you are within 15 yards, the air is filled with tension—tension that is completely self-created, of course, but tension nonetheless.

I had a situation like that. Had to do with water. I thought my neighbor's sump pump was draining a lot of water into my yard, turning the grass into a mini swamp. His position was that the drain pipe didn't extend past the fence, and he couldn't control where the water would settle. Suddenly, tension existed where none did before. It spilled over to our spouses, and we generally tried to avoid each other. Ridiculous, I know. After a couple of months, I happened to be driving by a famous New Jersey bakery, Mendokers', and decided it was time to turn over a new leaf. I bought a few apple turnovers and went next door, apologized and made a "let's put this behind us" offering. He accepted, and in short order, things were back to normal.

Now, the point of this story isn't what I did with the pastries, believe me. It's that we all can allow ourselves to be easily offended and become indignant and proud and dig in deeper—usually over something pretty insignificant, like a temporary wet lawn. And far more important than my peace offering was that my neighbor accepted it.

## Swallowing Your Pride Is Non-Fattening

Pride. It tops the list of the "seven deadly sins," and too much of it prevents us from ever getting to the "forgive" part of "forgive and forget." Of course, being proud and satisfied for what one has achieved is good. You should take pride in a strong work ethic, earning a college degree, staying fit, raising good kids or creating a chocolate empire! That's well-placed pride. It's when pride is misplaced that it becomes the problem. Watch out when you start becoming impressed with yourself (Messrs. Salt and Beauregarde, for example), or when years go by without saying "I'm sorry." Or you feel people owe you. You may think you're standing on principle, but be careful—you may be slipping on pride.

## morsels to munch on

◈ When you genuinely forgive, you will forget and there won't be regret.

◈ Beware of being easily offended.

◈ Being proud is good. Being prideful? Not so good.

# Lesson Nine

## Spare the Rod, Spoil the Veruka

*If you want children to keep their feet on the ground, put some responsibility on their shoulders.*

—Abigail Van Buren

"But Daddy, I want an Oompa Loompa now!"

That was one of the more memorable lines from the movie, delivered by the spoiled brat Veruka, the overindulged peanut heiress, and reflective of everything a child shouldn't be—disrespectful, disobedient and just plain nasty.

Probably not a surprise outcome. Veruka continually makes unreasonable demands because she has an inflated sense of who she is. She thinks she deserves an Oompa Loompa simply because she wants one. Her father is weak and promises to give her whatever she wants simply to shut her up! Still, she screams at him, "You don't love me!" She was quite skillful in manipulating her parents, and their "dereliction of duty" led to her becoming an imperious tyrant. Dr. Phil McGraw, psychologist, television host and author, advises parents, "Your primary job as a parent is to prepare your child for how the world really works. In the real world, you don't always get what you want. You will be better able to deal with that as an adult if you've experienced it as a child."

If it's not obvious from the heading and introduction, this is going to be the "parent chapter." If peace of mind is the real golden ticket, then for those of us with kids, developing the right relationship with them is a big piece of the peace. So, if you're not a parent, feel free to move on to the next chapter. But, if you are a parent or plan to have children in the future—or you're just curious—please stay!

## Love, Protect, Nurture, Enjoy

Love, protect, nurture, enjoy. I could be wrong, but I think that sums up what we should be doing as parents. Loving our children unconditionally. Defending them like a mama grizzly bear. Helping them grow into the mature, responsible, fully functioning adults they deserve to be. And enjoying them along the way.

A few thoughts on the subject.

## Let's Go Dutch

You'll recall the tale of the little Dutch boy, who, upon passing a dike on his way to school and seeing a small hole from which water leaked through, put his finger in it to prevent the sea from crashing in and destroying the town.

As parents, we need to show similar courage and keep our finger in the dike that holds back the sea of unwanted influences from television, peers, Internet and social media, as long as we can. Our children will be in the world soon enough, but it's never too soon to be vigilant about what we allow into our home or between our kid's ears.

## About Face... book

About face! Military jargon to pivot and face in the opposite direction from the original position. Not a bad thought when it comes to our kids and their social media consumption and how we're parenting about it. How many "friends" does one need on Facebook anyway?

Home used to be the impenetrable fortress. Once kids came home from a last round of evening play, the door closed behind them and the influence of the outside world was done for the day. The Internet didn't exist and TV was nowhere as insidious as it is now, In short, they were safe, and with you.

Of course, there is much good to Facebook and social media. Families and friends have a convenient way to stay connected, long lost relatives have been found, crimes have been solved, new products and businesses have been launched and rogue regimes around the world have toppled. But how much of a tween and teen's world should be consumed with it?

Like a salmon swimming upstream, it may be time for you to go against the current of cultural normal. Consider implementing some house rules like a "digital lights out" policy at 9:30 p.m. when there are no more cell phone calls, texts, Internet chats, Skyping, Face-booking, etc. If you've allowed the kids to drift off to sleep wearing those white earplugs and listening to music, maybe it's time to unplug them. Why? Because it's important for children to spend some time each day plugged into their own thoughts, instead of being continually fed the thoughts and ideas of someone else.

## You Are What You Tweet

Over time, the kind of food we choose to consume—to take in—will have an impact on how our bodies look, and more importantly, our overall level of health. There is much truth in the adage, "You are what you eat." It's certainly reflective in Augustus, who isn't helped much by his all-too-accommodating mother: "Eating is his hobby, you know. We encourage him. He wouldn't do it unless he needed the nourishment."

If we are what we eat, then we are what we tweet. If children's minds are continually filled with the thinking and values of everybody they "follow," it won't be an accident that they reflect, in dress, speech and attitude, what others deem desirable, and which you may not approve of. So, why are so many children consuming full bowls of no-nutrition social media with little parental oversight? Could be parents haven't thought about it in the proper context. Or some are lazy and, to the degree their kids are involved in social media, they don't have to be involved with them.

Whatever the case, it's never too late to choose a better course of action. If your child is on Facebook, are you a friend? If they are tweeting, are you following them? Does the "You" in YouTube not apply? "But they need their privacy," the culture says. Why? Kids still spend a lot of time away from their parents with friends at school, activities and social events. They have quite a bit of private time.

Maybe now is the time for an "about face" on Facebook, Twitter, and other media consumption for the kids. As enjoyable as it can be, there needs to be some "little Dutch boy" finger-in-the-dike oversight. How many hours does a 13 year old really need to spend on Facebook every week? Believe me, it's a question, not a judgment. I'm on your side because it's you against the world. You (and your children) are out-numbered, out-teched and out-shouted by the dominant media and so-called cultural norms. Do everything you can to level the playing field.

## But All My Friends Are Allowed to [Fill in the Blank]

A sign that you are dong the right thing. There's a reason you said no to a particular movie, a sleepover or a hanging-out event with some friends. Stay strong and try not to be swayed by your child's plea for fairness or even manipulation. ("I won't talk to you ever again. You're a rotten, mean father. You never give me any-thing I want." Guess who said that?) Or swayed by your misplaced guilt. Your rules may be different than those of the permissive majority, but it doesn't mean your rules are wrong.

You've got one shot at raising your children. And know something about their friends, too, as they can be strong influencers. It's a fact backed up by 25 years of research by Dr. David McClelland of Harvard. He concluded that the choice of a negative reference group is "in itself enough to condemn a person to failure and underachievement in life."

Here's a way to think about this "reference group" idea. Would your child become a better gymnast, soccer player, martial artist or ballerina if she practices and competes with those better than her, or less skilled? Most likely, she gets better and starts achieving higher levels of performance when surrounded by those more advanced in skills. She'll be inspired and will start to imitate the right techniques and moves and develop the best habits.

It follows that the same happens with one's circle of friends. If your child hangs out with the slackers, those who just get by, those who have a chip on their shoulder or those with behavior like the brats booted out of Wonka's factory—your kids will not be better off. Instead of evolving they will start devolving. So, let your kids choose their friends, but you choose them too!

## Trust but Verify

They say politics makes strange bedfellows, so it's not uncommon for governments to "trust, but verify" when dealing with each other. Good parenting advice, too. We should trust our children, and give them age-appropriate freedoms, but trust should be continually earned. As it is earned, more is given. But sometimes, it's okay to be a "benevolent dictator" and conduct a surprise inspection when you have some concerns.

We're parents—we know what we know. It's what we don't know that could be the cause of future problems.

## Just a Minute

There are a lot of them in a day. Minutes, that is. 1,440, to be exact. As parents, we've all told our kids "just a minute," genuinely meaning to help them in a moment or sometimes hoping that whatever is so important to them they forget, so we can continue doing whatever it is that is so important to us!

Just a minute here, and just a minute there eventually add up. To an hour. And hours add up to days. Days into years, years into decades and decades into a lifetime. So, without exaggerating, a minute can be a pretty important nurturing moment. Yet, we're always rushing around, filling in all the minutes with "busy." It's understandable that you've become a "minivan mamma or pappa," chauffeuring the kids back and forth to school, sports, ballet, piano lessons, karate and a dozen other activities. Doing things for our children is a sign of love. Preparing their meals, ironing clothes, chauffeuring, sewing a button, buying things. There's a certain momentum to it, and it's a beautiful thing. It means you are in the doing.

Have you thought about the "in the being" part? Being in the doing. It's challenging as life is on hyper speed, but that's where the hidden treasure lies. Being is the "just a minute" time—stopping and sitting for a few minutes to listen—completely—not while multi-tasking. Turning off the car radio during drive time to talk. Not lashing out in frustration, even though you're feeling very frustrated about something. In short, it's about committing to being present in your kids' emotional lives and not on the sidelines.

## Talk Is Not Cheap

It's golden. It's priceless, actually—talking with our children. In the late '90s, Bill Cosby hosted a show called "Kids Say the Darndest Things." He asked random questions to children, typically three to eight years old, and their answers were always very funny. But we don't need a show to know kids say the darndest things, because they are saying them right in our kitchens and living rooms, while driving in the car and before going to bed.

Beyond appreciating what can be priceless comments, we need to be engaged. The key to talking and engaging with our children versus at them is to listen. And to do so earnestly. The Chinese kanji *ting* represents the verb "to listen," and consists of the characters for ears, eyes and heart. How insightful—and instructional. Listening to our children is far more than just hearing what they say. It's active, it's our undivided attention and it's the basis for meaningful exchange.

When Charlie visited his mom at work, Mrs. Bucket sat down and listened undividedly to him. When we question why our teenagers don't talk to us anymore, maybe it's because we stopped listening to them a long time ago. Or, we just never did it much, and now it's awkward. However, it's never too late to start the conversation—and a good place to begin is with your ears, eyes and heart.

## Not Every Kid Deserves a Trophy

Not everyone is a winner. (Keep reading!) When one side wins the soccer game, the other side loses. Loses the game. There's nothing wrong with losing a game. But some parents (and coaches and teachers) have adopted an "everybody is a winner" philosophy because if little Johnny loses something, it will damage his self-esteem. (Maybe your self-esteem too?)

Wanting to build a child's self-esteem is good, because there is evidence that children who don't like themselves go on to have all sorts of behavioral issues. But it's not because they didn't get a gold ribbon or were not selected for the starting lineup, it's because they didn't feel loved or wanted. The best way to build your child's self-esteem is to love them unconditionally. Set the expectations bar high. You don't necessarily need to be a "tiger mother" like Amy Chua, but teaching your child that life is full of winning some and losing some is the best approach. Because that's what happens in real life. And the more children try, learn and become better for the experience, at the end of the day, they will have chalked up far more wins than losses. They may not have every trophy on the shelf, but the ones they do have will be far more meaningful.

Appropriate self-esteem building will help contribute to a positive, well-rounded and adjusted child. But over-the-top self-esteem building? Hello Veruka!

## Let Them Get Dirty, Jump in Puddles and Swing High on the Swing, But Make Sure They Brush Their Teeth!

You've probably heard of today's helicopter parents—hovering close to the kids to keep them safe. (I'm one of them. Maybe you are too.) But we've got to be reasonable—we don't want to rob them (and us!) of what a childhood should be—full of fun, imagination, exploration and learning from mistakes, to name a few things. When they swing high and you get a little nervous they could get hurt—but you see the excitement and accomplishment on their face—let them swing high anyway, despite your anxiety. And they're not in imminent danger when occasionally bike riding without a helmet. Chances are they won't get a cold running outside in the rain. If they find themselves riding a Wonkavator… well, let's forget that one!

But when it comes to enforcing some non-negotiable "rules of the house," like brushing their teeth twice a day—that's something all together different. As parents, it's an expectation on our part that requires a little discipline on theirs. And to the degree we inspect what we expect on some of the little things, it will carry over to the bigger, more important ones. To the degree we don't, not only may tooth brushing suffer, but other things could as well.

This may be a stretch, but I liken this to the broken-windows theory. The idea was introduced in 1982 by social scientists James Wilson and George Kelling. They advanced that a successful strategy for preventing vandalism is to fix problems when they are small. In other words, repair the broken windows quickly, and the likelihood that vandals will do further damage decreases significantly.

Same with our kids. We need to give them room to explore, learn, make mistakes and be kids. But when it comes to the important, meaningful rules that are broken, just like the windows, we need to address them quickly before a tendency develops to break more of them.

## Catch 'Em in the Act

No, not in breaking the rules, but catch your kid "in the act" of doing something good. When he stays up late to study for a test. Unloads the dishwasher, unasked. Or goes out of his way to help a friend, despite its being inconvenient. Behaviors that you recognize and appropriately praise have a tendency to repeat themselves.

## The Closing Window of Opportunity

Realize that from the moment your baby is placed in your arms, the window of opportunity—to impress upon them your values, your thinking and your beliefs—starts to close. It happens slowly at first, but over time the window is going to close. It's also a time to truly appreciate that our children are a gift from God, a precious, temporary gift that we are given responsibility for loving, raising appropriately and enjoying.

There are no guarantees, of course, but by being thankful and present for this gift, and by being loving, vigilant, nurturing and responsible parents, we minimize the likelihood of raising a child with an "I want an Oompa Loompa now!" attitude, or worse.

## Don't Outgrow Your Children

One final thought. When it comes to outgrowing your children, just *don't* do it. Period. (Sorry, Nike.)

### morsels to munch on

- ◈ Love, protect, nurture and enjoy your children.

- ◈ Remain vigilant in keeping out the unwanted influences of the culture.

- ◈ Love unconditionally and the self-esteem stuff takes care of itself.

# Lesson Ten

## Peace of Mind: The Real Golden Ticket

*If there is to be any peace it will come
through being, not having.*

—Henry Miller

A frenzied, worldwide search begins when Wonka announces that a lifetime supply of chocolate will be given to five golden ticket holders. Those looking for the elusive golden ticket think that by winning one, satisfaction, happiness and contentment will follow. After all, this is Wonka chocolate, considered the most delicious and desirable of all confections. How could such a treasure not keep one happy for a lifetime?

A parallel to Wonka's golden ticket is the multi-state mega lotteries we spoke about in Lesson Two. Once the jackpot gets big enough, long lines into convenience stores can been seen for blocks, hopefuls trying to get their shot at the prize before the drawing. Local reporters on the scene ask the predictable "What will you do if you win?" question. Everyone is giddy and fantasizing about what they would do "if just this once." It's fun to fantasize about winning millions of dollars; I occasionally do it myself when I throw a buck at a jackpot (although I won't wait in a line any longer than three people).

By virtue of the graveyards of "stuff" that lie in our homes, it's not just a grand prize that we think will make us happy. It's seen in closets bursting at the seams with "I gotta have this" sweaters, blouses and belts, basements stacked with shoeboxes of "I can't live without these" heels and boots and garages filled with "I really need this" tools, still in their unopened packaging.

As we come to the final pages in this book, I want to share some ideas and thinking outside of the metaphorical backdrop of the movie that have been helpful for me—with the hope that they may have some relevance for you and your peace of mind.

## Serenity Now!

When we realize that serenity or tranquility is a key ingredient of contentment and inner calm, like most things, we want it immediately! I'm reminded of an episode from the comedy series *Seinfeld,* where George's father Frank is advised to calmly and reassuringly say "Serenity now" when he feels his blood pressure going up—but instead he yells it loudly, effectively doing more harm than good. Like Frank Costanza, we sometimes are our own worst enemy. We can't force serenity upon ourselves, just like we can't force peace of mind. But we can, and should, actively engage in thinking and pursuits that will provide a gateway for both.

## A Fix You Don't Need

It's good to want things. It's when the wants, be they material or emotional, are fillers for something missing in our lives that they become a fulfillment fix, a temporary high. That's when we need to change our mindset from "I want" to "Do I really want, or even need?"

Lasting peace of mind can never be purchased at retail, found in the blue eyes of Mr. Charming, gained from a McMansion or realized in that promotion to the executive suite. We see examples all too often of the beautiful, rich and famous who seemingly have it all but end up with shattered lives. We probably all know some beautiful and rich (but not so famous) people who end up in the same place too.

I'm focusing on the extremes here, but I hope you see the point. Temporary highs are just that. They have to be chased, and once captured, they soon lose their appeal when a newer, more exciting and interesting one surfaces. As Yogi Berra said, "It's like déjà-vu, all over again."

## Raising Your Peace-of-Mind Baseline

If we could measure our peace of mind with a graph, similar to how stocks are observed, we would see our baseline, how we are most of the time. A new relationship, promotion or the purchase of clothes electronic gadgets, jewelry or a new car, may cause the line to spike temporarily, but inevitably, it will go back down to the baseline.

The key to having lasting peace of mind is to not to chase the spikes, but to raise the baseline. It's true that a leopard can't change its spots. But we're humans—we can change how we act and interpret the world around us so we are more mindful and appreciative—so we embrace what is truly meaningful and lasting.

New baselines are created all the time in sports, music, academics, the arts, etc. When Roger Bannister broke the 4-minute-mile barrier in 1954, he shattered a psychological limitation and created a new baseline for that event. Danica Patrick became the first woman to win an Indycar Series title in 2008. The Guinness Book of World Records showcases new records (i.e., baselines) with each year's publication. And there are countless more.

The point is, wherever your peace-of-mind baseline is now, you can change it, if you want to. But it's a choice. It won't magically raise on its own, like the rising sea. It takes some mental and emotional effort.

## Discovering Peace of Mind: Random Thoughts on Weeds, Drill Instructors, Laundry, Carpet and a Couple of Movies

I'm pleased where my baseline is. "Getting here" has been shaped in part by the blessings of great parents and a wonderful childhood. But the larger part is deliberate. We all make choices. We choose every thought, every emotion, every act... we really do. And I appreciate the unfairness of life and its difficulties and what trauma and hardships can do. It makes it more difficult to choose how we are going to be. But in the end, it's always up to us.

Abraham Lincoln said, "People are just as happy as they make up their minds to be." That doesn't mean happiness magically happens when you decide to make up your mind with the morning bed. But, it's the starting point. And everything begins with a starting point. So with that as an introduction, random thoughts, here we go!

## Got Weeds?

Why does maintaining a plush green lawn or beautiful flower garden require effort—planting, fertilizing, watering and sunlight—but weeds grow with no effort at all? And, when not controlled, a landscape once beautiful and tranquil becomes ugly and distressed. It's the same with us. We need to take in the mental equivalent of fertilizer, water and sunlight to ensure the weeds of negative thinking, attitude and emotion don't take root internally and turn our peace of mind into shattered pieces of mind.

If it were possible to call a landscape supply store and order a personalized sack of mental fertilizer, what would be in it? How would the mix of things we do, friends we keep, promises we make, books we read, conversations we have and predominant thoughts we hold, compare to what we're currently doing?

Remember, weeds weigh us down. Weeds are things like simmering over the rude behavior of a customer service rep, remaining offended by a friend's snub or being jealous of a colleague's success. When that happens, it's time to use our mental weed-killer spray! Process the information a little differently. Just think, we'll never deal with that customer service person again, our friend was probably just not herself at that moment and our promotion will come one day too.

## You Can Never Do Anything Fast Enough for Your Drill Instructor

As the Greyhound bus pulled into the base after midnight and slowly crept by the dimly lit United States Marine Corps Recruit Depot sign, two intimidating drill instructors sprinted out of the receiving building and one boarded the bus. I'll never forget the first words I heard spoken in Paris Island, South Carolina. Out from the raspy-voiced drill instructor came the words, "You are now property of the United States Government!"

The break-down, build-up process of military boot camp, and in particular, the U.S. Marine Corps, is fairly well known, as it is widely depicted in movies, television and books. Still, being the one subjected to it makes all the difference, and at the end of the first week, it's hard not to believe that you are the most incompetent recruit who has ever set foot on the island.

Fortunately, attending religious services is allowed, and after a week of training I was happy to be in church for observance, to say nothing of the joy of sitting for an hour without being yelled at. Most importantly, the pastor shared some advice that helped me immeasurably over the next 11 weeks, not to mention the past 25 years. "Recruits," he said, "you can never do anything fast enough for your drill instructor." Wow! You can never do anything fast enough for your drill instructor. I realized that nothing I did during boot camp would please my drill instructor, but that I should—and would—continue to push myself to excel, regardless of how it would be perceived or appreciated.

In boot camp, there is a method to the madness—tear down to build up. But in the ordinary world, we all encounter people—a boss, neighbor, colleague, teacher, even a loved one—where we will never do anything fast enough or fill-in-the-blank enough for them. These people thrive on the tear down, not the build up. Whether their behavior is deliberate or a character flaw, the key for us is to just accept it as an immutable and unchanging fact.

Psychologist, author and radio host Dr. Joy Browne offers the advice that we can't control other people, but we can always control how we react to them. Isn't that empowering? Thus, we should continue to do our best for us, not them. You will always appreciate your own hard work.

## Laundry Days and Mondays
## Never Get Me Down

It's how you look at things. When we "have" to get up early on Monday and go back to work, it means we've got work to go back to. And bemoaning that unending parade of pants, pajamas, polos and pullovers that mysteriously march their way into the hamper fails to appreciate that we're doing laundry not just for ourselves, but for others living with us too. Which means we're not alone. For me, it's a reminder that my kids are still young and at home—a situation that is going to change soon, much too soon.

So, when laundry days and Mondays are getting you down, think about the whys behind the PJs you're folding or the early morning ringing of the alarm clock. It won't hurt either if you sing or hum that famous song from Karen Carpenter, with a slight change in the refrain!

## The Beauty of Worn Out Carpet

We could have replaced it some time ago. It's just that the tuition bills for our kids' Catholic grammar and high school come along pretty regularly. It's an investment my wife and I are happy to make, but there isn't much leftover for things like replacing some worn out carpet. We'll get to it soon enough—for now, though, it's a reminder that we're making a choice to put off some short-term nice-to-haves for long-term need-to-haves. I'll admit, there are days when the carpet looks less beautiful than others, but because our "doing" is aligned with our "believing," it's a sacrifice that helps us keep our peace of mind.

## I Think I Love My Wife

He does, of course, love his wife—and fortunately realizes it before it's too late. But in the movie by the same name, Chris Rock struggles as Richard Cooper, a middle-aged man who thinks his life has become predictable, routine and boring. He feels "trapped" by his marriage, two kids, house in the suburbs and career as an investment banker.

Then out of nowhere Nikki shows up, a friend from the past who just happens to be beautiful, interesting and exciting. She doesn't hold back from letting Richard know she is interested in being more than a friend. Eventually the flirtations lead to a point and a place where Richard is within seconds of making a very bad decision. A reflection of himself in a mirror triggers a flashback to a moment at play with his son, and upon realizing the cliff he is about to jump over, he quite literally turns and runs.

This was Richard Cooper, but could just as easily been Rachel Cooper and the movie called I Think I Love My Husband. Life was boring. Why? Because the dominant culture, through movies, songs and imagery, mock it. House in the suburbs, the white picket fence, the lovely wife and the nice, well-adjusted kids... Who wants that? the culture tells us. But don't buy into that mockery, or you will most likely be trading temporary disappointment for long-term disaster.

## It's a Wonderful Life

It's probably in everyone's top three favorite Christmas movies of all time. George Bailey, who has been battling the evil Mr. Potter from taking over the Bailey Savings & Loan, reaches a boiling point where he is contemplating suicide, assuming that his wife, kids and other people he loves would be better off if he were dead. On a snowy Christmas Eve, when he is prepared to throw himself off a bridge, his guardian angel appears and grants him his wish—to see what the world would be like without him in it. In short, he sees it is not a better place—that he made a difference. And that he's had a wonderful life.

It's the same for us. Our lives are probably far more wonderful than we all realize. An "acre of diamonds" could be buried right under our feet for the taking. We just need to see, and appreciate, what's beyond the surface.

## morsels to munch on

◈ Raise your peace-of-mind baseline, and chasing temporary highs will look far less appealing.

◈ Don't allow the mental equivalent of weeds to take hold of your thinking.

◈ You can't control others, but you can always control how you react to them.

◈ There is probably a life's acre of diamonds, right under your feet, if you look beyond your surface.

# Conclusion

The promise of this book was that you would find something satisfying inside it—a nugget of wisdom, an insight, some encouragement, a reminder of what's meaningful. Nuggets to nibble on versus some long, drawn-out definitive treatise on how to live, be happy or achieve peace of mind. Because a nugget may be just what you need right now, at this very moment—to temporarily satisfy a hunger pang in your life, help realize your blessings or provide some pick-me-up inspiration to "get out of bed" and "buy another chocolate bar."

Although this book has an introduction and con-clusion, it's not a linear story—you can jump in and out as you would like and need to. Maybe one read will "hit the spot" for you. Perhaps reflecting on a chapter or writing down a morsel to munch on (or two!) on an index card and referring to it occasionally will be useful. Trying out just one idea could make a big difference.

I'm just like you—trying to navigate through life, do my best for my family, live the right way and enjoy the journey. I don't have all the answers, but I've come across a few. Hopefully, some I've shared in these pages will work for you.

As the chocolate factory tour began, Wonka told his guests, "It's nice to have you here. I'm so glad you could come. This is going to be such an exciting day. I hope you enjoy it. I think you will."

I feel the same way as our "tour" comes to an end. It's been nice to have you here, reading this book, and I hope you have found a few nuggets worth nibbling on, ones that are rich and purposeful and that really will make a long and lasting difference in your life, far beyond the first bite.

# morsels to munch on

## A Review

### Lesson 1. Moments of Decision

- ◈ Base decisions on principles, not circumstances. Principles don't change.

- ◈ Beware of the "butterfly effect" that comes with every decision.

- ◈ You can run, and you can hide—but not from consequences.

### Lesson 2. All I Have to Do Is Dream—Not!

- ◈ Wake up! Dreaming is the starting point, not the staying point.

- ◈ Don't break the law—of attraction (but don't count on it entirely).

- ◈ A dollar and a dream is not a good plan to invest in.

## Lesson 3. Get Out of Bed!

◈ Throw off the covers of fear and get out of bed!

◈ Remember, today *is* tomorrow.

◈ Dissatisfied? Good! Now be inspirationally dissatisfied.

◈ Pay the price today for what you want, and you will never suffer from buyer's remorse.

## Lesson 4. If at First You Don't Succeed, Buy Another Chocolate Bar

◈ Failure is only in the act, never in the person.

◈ Be a meaningful specific versus a wandering generality!

◈ Eavesdrop on your own internal dialogue—what are you saying?

◈ Play to your natural strengths, talents and abilities. You will stay motivated—and chalk up more wins than losses.

## Lesson 5. The Good Can Be Bad and Ugly

❖ Who do you want "to be or not to be"?
  That is the question.

❖ Develop the habit of asking yourself, "Is this
  a wise decision?"

❖ Open your emotional and mental door to
  life's good things knocking at it.

## Lesson 6. Revenge Is Never Sweet

❖ Let go of the grudge.

❖ Get rid of "get even" thinking—immediately.

❖ There is no upside to revenge. None.

## Lesson 7. The Good Humor Man or Woman

❖ You don't have to be the funny one to have
  a good sense of humor.

❖ Laughter can be the best medicine to treat a
  difficult situation.

❖ Smiling is one of the few things that the
  more you give it away, the more it comes
  back to you.

## Lesson 8. Forgive and Forget... Regret

◈ When you genuinely forgive, you will forget and there won't be regret.

◈ Beware of being easily offended.

◈ Being proud is good. Being prideful? Not so good.

## Lesson 9. Spare the Rod, Spoil the Veruka

◈ Love, protect, nurture and enjoy your children.

◈ Remain vigilant in keeping out the unwanted influences of the culture.

◈ Love unconditionally and the self-esteem stuff takes care of itself.

## Lesson 10. Peace of Mind:
## The Real Golden Ticket

❖ Raise your peace-of-mind baseline, and chasing temporary highs will look far less appealing.

❖ Don't allow the mental equivalent of weeds to take hold of your thinking.

❖ You can't control others, but you can always control how you react to them.

❖ There is probably a life's acre of diamonds, right under your feet, if you look beyond your surface.

# Acknowledgments

Many thanks to those who provided valuable feedback on the manuscript—Ted Haverkost, Al Holl (my brother), Albert Holl (my father), Jeff Hoyak, Susan Koval, Janet Madigan, Laura Riccardi, Linda Richardson, Lynette Smith and Kimberly Stillman.

CPSIA information can be obtained at www.ICGtesting.com
Printed in the USA
BVOW081334290612

294006BV00004B/1/P